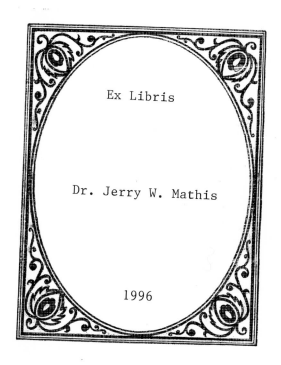

Ex Libris

Dr. Jerry W. Mathis

1996

WHOM DO I HAVE
THE HONOUR OF
ADDRESSING?

WHOM DO I HAVE THE HONOUR OF ADDRESSING?

A Play by
Peter Shaffer

First presented on BBC Radio
on November 20 1989 by
Dame Judi Dench

ANDRE DEUTSCH

First published 1990 by
André Deutsch Limited
105-106 Great Russell Street WC1B 3LJ

British Library Cataloguing in Publication Data

Shaffer, Peter, *1926-*
  Whom do I have the honour of addressing?
  I. Title
  822.914

ISBN 0 233 98615 4

Printed and bound in Great Britain
by WBC Bridgend and Maesteg

For Anne and Sherban
with love

INTRODUCTION
by the Author

Speaking generally, I have always been depressed by the prospect of seeing a play with only two characters. I read the programme and unavoidably think 'Dreary: no one else is going to appear.' There are of course wonderous exceptions – notably Beckett's *Happy Days* and the no less remarkable *Two Character Play* of Tennessee Williams, which I was fortunate enough to read in manuscript before it seemed to get re-written out of its pristine excellence – but in the main three seems to be the minimum number of characters a playwright can unmonotonously succeed with: unless, paradoxically, he writes a piece with just one.

Strangely, the one-character play does not generate in one's mind the same gloomy expectation. On the stage at this moment it actually seems to be more popular than it has ever been – which is fortunate, since the economics of the theatre dictate its appearance with ever-increasing insistence.

The dramatic monologue, of course, is an age-honoured form. In the fabled days of live home entertainment it flourished richly, sustaining generations of eager uncles and reluctant nieces, and alternately delighting and boring countless family audiences. Nowadays, when it appears that technology and timidity between them have ensured that no amateur can creditably recite in public any more (or in fact offer anything very much in the way of entertainment which is actually self-produced) the solo turn in its dramatic shape has entirely disappeared from the living room – except on television screens and, of course, radio, where thankfully it has never died.

Obviously the attractions of radio monologue for the playwright are manifold. So much less stands between the writer and the embodiment of his work. There are no vast expenses involved in producing it; no tense conferences with stage designers or casting advisors; no weeks of doubt-filled auditions or months of urgent telephone talks with producers. Even meetings with the director are liable to be short and to the point. You write it – then you do it: it's apt to be as simple as that.

'Whom Do I Have The Honour of Addressing?' was actually recorded by the B.B.C. on two successive days, with the most pleasing absence of fuss. Judi Dench, having read and approved the script, arrived briskly at the studio on a Thursday morning and read it through without stopping to the highly professional ears of the director, Glynn Dearman, absorbing the nuances of the material as she went along. Thereupon she immediately recorded it for transmission, in nine separate sections. She acted two versions of each section – that is, until the closing pages, when she was enabled by her astonishing technique to bring off the last desperate scenes in one unerring attempt. I sat in awe of her passionate involvement and brilliant dramatic intelligence. By Friday noon it was all achieved – seventy-five minutes of virtuosity and increasing pain – and there she was on tape: Angela Parsons, ex-director of Swift Scripts Ltd. of Wardour Street – practical and romantic, so clear-eyed and so deluded, funny and moving and alive.

Perversely, I now have to admit that I am contemplating a presentation of this play on the stage. I suppose I am first and foremost a theatre person: I like to see audiences, and feel the electric charge of their concentration galvanising a performance into a life it could not achieve in any other medium. This said, however, I remain profoundly grateful to the B.B.C. – and most especially to Mr Dearman – for presenting my piece with such experienced skill. They reminded me in their dedication that there is and will always remain a kind of private truth which can only be fully made manifest in the most austere and uncompromising of all histrionic forms – the sound broadcast. I hope to repeat this whole experience very soon.

Peter Shaffer

WHOM DO I HAVE
THE HONOUR OF
ADDRESSING?

PLACE: The living room of a second-floor flat in Clapham, London.

TIME: Now.

[*Angela, an Englishwoman in her fifties, sits by a tape recorder.*]

[*Music fades in: 'When you wish upon a star' in the lush Melachrino arrangement. It fades out as Angela begins to speak.*]

First things first. Press button marked 'Record' . . . Such a *final* word. What I need to be *now*. Final . . . Record.

[*She presses the 'Record' button and speaks carefully into the machine*]

Hallo . . . Hallo . . . Hallo . . . Whom . . . Whom . . . Whom . . . Whom do I have the honour of addressing?

[*She stops the tape and winds it back. The sound of its babble is heard loudly. Then she stops it.*]

And play . . .

[*She presses the 'Play' button and the tape repeats her voice:*]

'Hallo . . . Hallo . . . Hallo . . . Whom . . . Whom . . . Whom . . . Whom do I have the honour of addressing?'

[*She stops it.*]

Good. Such a little thing to do such damage — one tiny tape . . . Well then now — we begin. Turn, little tape. Record! For posterity.

[*She presses the 'Record' button again. Speaking into it*]

Hallo, Posterity. This is Eleven Dawlish Road, Clapham, London. Thursday evening, March the whatever. You are about to hear the only statement ever made by me, Mrs Angela Parsons, concerning her life. Emendation: her life and death . . . No doubt the latter will be of considerably more interest, especially to those people who make their living from scandals. Journalists and so forth. Our charitable press . . . And certainly, *to one other person*, most especially.

[*Pause*]

This tape is by way of being a little time bomb. Scheduled to explode tomorrow, or perhaps the next day, — depending on when one is found. Certainly when one is no longer around to hear the bang . . . A pity in a way, but unavoidable. The special other person will certainly hear it — loud and clear. And so will hundreds of younger people. Actually, thousands, Even millions. Think of that: millions of outraged, agonised teenagers! . . .

[*She laughs*]

Excuse me. This will make sense much more if you keep listening to this tape. It is intended to reach the widest possible audience.

4

[*Pause*]

Next things first: meaning whisky. My first taste of it ever, if you can believe this of a fifty-plus-year-old woman. White Horse Scotch . . . The noises you will hear intermittently as this tape turns will be me swallowing it. Apparently it is the best to go with other time bombs. I mean the ten little white ones in this bottle . . . First, it seems, one has to drink quite a lot of this stuff. So here goes. A first experience on a last day!

[*She drinks and gives a splutter of distaste.*]

Oh, good heavens − it's ghastly! Absolutely vile! . . . How on earth can people drink this for pleasure? The human race never ceases to amaze one . . . One more sip now − Oh, good God!

[*Another splutter*]

Oh − it's so strong! Why couldn't it just be white wine? A nice pleasant Orvieto? . . . I suppose that wouldn't work. After all, wine's a life-giver.

[*Pause*]

The tape's just turning there, round and round. Look at it − relentless: just like a spool of film. That's an excellent symbol of Life, a spool turning relentlessly. A most appropriate image in my case − as you will see. Let me plunge right in, with that 'Whom' I started with. That sentence − 'Whom do I have the honour of addressing?' That's where it all began, after all. The first sounds out of

5

his mouth. So utterly unexpected. I mean utterly for an American of twenty-four years old. They don't say 'Whom' at the best of times, Americans — they have no grammar — and there he was, this almost-boy still, smiling away at me with that dimple, which is a world-famous feature in its own right by now, saying it to me, clear as anything: 'whom'!

Connie said he was sending me up. She was my partner then — nine months ago: it all seems so much longer. We ran the agency together — Swift Scripts Limited in Wardour Street, the most efficient typing firm in London for plays and films. A rather embittered woman, who thinks her life's mission is to take people down a peg . . . I'm sorry, Connie, but that's true . . . I said, 'Well, what if he was? I deserved it. I had no right to say what I did in front of everyone.' But she said [*prissy voice*] 'Rubbish! If film stars expect to be clapped and cheered from morning till night, they've got to take the risk of somebody giving them a taste of reality now and again.'

Actually I hadn't intended to do any such thing. It was the coat made me do it – that awful fur . . . You must picture the scene for a moment. A thousand people, including me, waiting on the kerb outside the Odeon Cinema, Leicester Square — and him suddenly standing there in front of me — Tom Prance himself — with that famous dimple and his skin so much more beautiful than it even is in films! And then that joke fur coat, three sizes too big, trailing on the ground behind him like it was on Marlene Dietrich — or

Mae West, that was much more the picture — Mae West. I couldn't help myself. I shouted out — 'You look horrible!' And he stopped dead in his tracks. The crowd all leaned forward to listen. He stared at me in absolute amazement — and then he bowed! Just like a cavalier in a history epic à la *Three Musketeers* — and spoke that ridiculous sentence in a high-falutin' voice: 'Whom do I have the honour of addressing?'

It was astounding. I mean, he could have said something much nastier, like, 'Who on earth are *you*?' or 'How do you dare?' Because, after all, he must have spent most of his preceding five years having flattering things said to him every minute by young girls, not being called 'horrible' by a middle-aged woman in a mac . . . He took it so well — that's what I'm really saying. It just caught my heart.

It's actually why I wrote him to California. If I'd thought about it for two seconds, I never would have. I mean, the odds alone of a letter even reaching him were so slim! Everyone knows that stars don't read their own letters: that's left to Personal Assistants . . . Come to think of it — why didn't Bud open it, and not he? If that isn't Fate, what is? . . .

Anyway, let me say it all in order. We're standing in Leicester Square and he's in that offensive coat. 'I guess you must be an Animal Rights person,' he says. 'Well, if

7

it's the fur that's bugging you, it's fake — so don't worry about it.'

'I'm not at all worried,' I reply. 'I don't give a hoot about animals.'

'Are you kidding?' he says. 'How can anyone not care about animals?'

'Because I'm tired of them,' I say. 'They're on television every single night. All those insects with their life-cycles done to classical music. And those choosy little things who only eat bamboo or eucalyptus. I'm sick to death of them all!'

Actually I didn't mean any of it. I had no idea why I said it. But he laughed anyway, and then went on in his silly Cavalier's voice:

'Well, if it isn't animals, My Lady, what is the source of your objection to this elegant coat?' And I said '*skin!*' . . . Well, in for a penny, in for a pound! — 'You've got the best skin in the whole film industry,' I said. 'I saw your top half in *Crackerjack* and your altogether in *Flame-man*, and it really is stupid to cover that all up in fur — fake or not. It's like hiding God's gift.'

'Well,' he says, 'you don't expect me to come to a première stark naked, do you?' And I say, if you can believe it! — 'Why not? I don't see that being the source of *anyone's* objection!' . . . I could have bitten off my tongue the second I said it — but he really roared with laughter.

And then the Manager of the cinema came out in an evening dress with a ghastly mauve frilled shirt, and spoke in a tone I can only call 'veiled menace': 'Excuse me, Mr Prance, but you are very late, and Her Royal Highness *is* waiting.' The poor boy jumped as if he'd been shot — grabbed my hand — said, 'Oops — goodbye!' and bolted inside. The Manager gave me a look of what was meant to be cold *hauteur*, and followed at a stately pace.

I entirely admit I'd gone too far: — but still, all the crowd was looking at me with undisguised envy. Some of them knew me, of course. I am, after all, something of a human landmark outside cinemas at premières. 'Alas,' as Connie would say . . . She's a great Alasser is my ex-partner. Along with everybody else who knows me, she always thought it appalling, my addiction to films. [*prissy voice*] 'However can you do it?' she'd say. 'A woman of your years standing for hours in the rain, just to see some Californian nitwit step out of a hired Daimler.' There was no explaining it to her . . . Any more than there is explaining this, what I'm doing now. Everyone I know is going to say, 'Oh dear — things really ran away with her this time! What a perfectly insane thing to do!' . . . I'm sorry: I can't help it. That's all one can reply.

9

[*Pause*]

A personal insert here, to you, Connie. You'll be especially horrified when you hear the news, I realise that. I can only hope that after hearing this tape you'll be a little on my side. However, if you're not — frankly, I don't much care. Honestly. This is the way I am now, Connie. No longer the Angela you knew — if you ever did . . . Still, I do apologise to you for one thing. I'm sorry I left you in the lurch that way, three months ago, just as the business was really starting to thrive.

That must have left a lot of work for you. Please try to understand, though. Even now — when it has all turned out so disastrously — I have to tell you: for someone like me there has finally to be something more in life than being the most flourishing Proprietress of a Typing Agency. I'd have left it all anyway, sooner or later. Five consecutive years of Clapham and Wardour Street, with two weeks of Torquay thrown in each September, had me absolutely 'stir-crazy', as the Americans say. Not 'star-crazy', Connie, as you called me; 'stir-crazy'. Meaning going steadily bonkers because of the dreariness. I just didn't realise how bad it was till he entered my life . . .

[*Pause. Again she drinks — and again coughs with disgust*]

Oh! . . . The point about Leicester Square is that I had never in my whole life talked to a human being like that, let alone a Film Star. I'm not actually one of those fans who makes any outward show of her admiration. Nor am I remotely given to that kind of rudeness and even — I admit it — lewdness . . . It's why I wrote to him. And

Hollywood — and hoped for the best. I was absolutely astounded when he actually wrote back three weeks later. I could hardly read the letter, the words were dancing so much. Beautifully formed words too, like Sunday School writing. I have it here as well. It has been in my wallet since the day it came. The folds are almost torn through by now . . .

[*She takes it out most carefully*]

It said . . .

[*Reading*]

Dear Angela Parsons,

It was great to get your letter. It was so sincere and honest, and I really appreciate that. Please do not worry about what you said to me in Leicester Square — it was spelt L-E-S-T-E-R — that coat truly is terrible. Actually I concede something too: it is the pits! And I even know what you mean about too many animal movies on TV. There is a whole slew of them I keep viewing on P.B.S., and I have to ask myself, 'Have I seen this one before?' . . . P.S. Please write to me again if you ever feel the urge. P.S. two. What are 'fulminations'?

[*Pause*]

I looked up 'pits' and 'slew' in an American dictionary, but it didn't contain them. So that actually gave me the excuse to reply — after a discreet couple of weeks so as not to appear pestering. And I told him what my word meant:

'fulminations'. Also — partly I admit due to the influence of some Orvieto white wine I'd had at the Gondola restaurant in Carrington Gardens — I made my tone rather more personal.

[*She unfolds another letter. Reading*]

Dear Tom,

Please forgive the celerity with which I reply, but it is really such a pleasure for me to write to you. It is the most brilliant night here in Clapham. The moonlight is simply pouring down like milk out of a bottle, all over Dawlish Road. Usually it is a grim road — too much sooty red brick — but tonight it is all gleaming. And my heart is gleaming too. It is what they used to call 'aglow'. 'Hearts aglow!' — what a lovely phrase! . . . I'm looking at your photograph. It is propped up behind the pencil-jar on my desk, torn out of one of those vulgar film magazines, but the picture is so charming I couldn't resist. It's the one of you standing in front of the Rehabilita- tion Centre in Birmingham on your visit to this country, wearing armour and holding up the card you'd designed: the one which says, 'Slay The Dragon of Drugs!'. Anyone else would have looked ridiculous doing that, but you do not at all! . . . There is such a thing as 'shining sincerity' — it can take us anywhere we wish to go — and yours is as visible and wonderful as any I have ever encountered.

Of all causes to take up, Drugs surely is the most urgent of our time. And only someone

like you can really help. You are a Hero to the
Young, and they will actually listen to
you! . . . I read that article about you in our
newspaper, *The Guardian*, describing the Rehabilitation Centre you set up in Los Angeles,
and I was really moved. God bless you, I say.
Don't ever let anyone mock you out of doing
the clean, right action . . . That's who you
are, Mr T. Prance: the Clean Right Fellow,
and I send you my most admiring wishes.

[*Pause*]

That's how it began: the Angela Parsons-Tom Prance
Correspondence! The incredible thing was that he wrote
back *again*! And in actual handwriting! − that same
Sunday School script − tracing the word 'celerity',
which I'd used, about fifty times to make a border . . . I
received four letters from him in all. And he must have
had twenty-four from me. Because I admit that once I
began, the tap was really turned on. It was as if one had
found an ideal correspondent. Someone who was far more
modern and With-It than one was oneself − and yet
wholesome as well. Not cynical or impatient with older
people, as the young mostly are. And not hippy or
pretentious.

Of course I was excessive in my replies. It's obvious as I
think about it − I'm an excessive personality. Just like that
time outside the cinema, I was taken over! I 'went on', as
they say. Pages and pages − from silly things like my
views on films, to actually discussing weighty World
Problems! . . . I kept copies of these too. I read them over
earlier this evening, and I wish I hadn't now, because they

helped to harden my decision . . . I suppose that's one of the worst experiences you can have − reading letters you once wrote to someone, heart aglow, knowing how it was all going to be treated later . . . Excuse me again.

[*She drinks more whisky*]

Anyway, there were no more letters from him, because the spoken word suddenly took over between us! . . . I'll never forget the morning he telephoned the office in Wardour Street. He must have looked it up in the book. I remember it was a Friday and I was typing a film script about a Bank Robbery: it was extremely boring, with nothing to sustain a typist's interest as she ploughed her way through it. And suddenly Connie calls over to me across the room, right over the heads of all our employees: 'Tom Prance is on the phone. He's asking for you! Personally! By name!'

Everybody stopped working.

'Who?' I say. I hear my voice actually leap an octave, and I feel myself going red right up to my temples. I try my best to sound really puzzled as I pick up the phone − and of course they're all listening to every word. When I speak, it's like one of those highly-charged conversations in a classic film thriller − like Barbara Stanwyck and Fred MacMurray in *Double Indemnity*.

'Whom am I addressing?' I say. I leave out 'the honour', of course − that would give the game away. No one would say that unless they knew the person. He still laughed down the phone and said, 'This is Sir Thomas Prance, Knight of the Fur Coat, at your service.' 'Oh yes,' I say, very formal, as if talking about a script he wants typed: 'that can be arranged. You'd have to choose what kind of a cover.' And he replies − quick as anything, clearly re-membering our conversation from outside the Odeon − 'Skin! I want a skin cover − I'll send some round!'

To this I can think of nothing to reply, and I'm sure my own skin is exactly like a traffic light! And then he says: 'I'm at the Savoy Hotel for three days. How's about brunch, day after tomorrow?' I just remember in time that brunch is what Hollywood people call Sunday lunch. 'That would be fine,' I say. 'No problem, Mr Prance. Thank you. Indeed. Absolutely.' And I hang up.

Connie is beside herself with curiosity. She comes rushing over like a madwoman, hissing in what she imagines is a Lowered Voice. 'Was that him? Was that really *him*?'

'Of course,' I say, as coolly as possible. 'I told you we met at a première. I must have given him our business card.'

'But what did he want? . . What on earth could he poss-ibly *want*?'

'A script typed, of course,' I say loftily. 'What else would he want? . . . I'm going to collect it over the weekend from his hotel.'

Her face is absolutely puckered with jealousy — she can hardly keep it out of her voice. 'But why doesn't he just send a messenger?' she says. It comes out of her almost like a shriek.

'Mine is not to reason why.' I reply. 'Oh, good heavens, it's lunch time!' And I rise and leave the room with my packet of banana sandwiches to eat on a bench in Soho Square, as is my wont. I have to admit that it was not a very collected exit. It actually needed what film directors would call another take.

[*Pause*]

I went to Regent Street the next day and bought myself a completely new outfit. A beige sweater and a very attractive skirt with brown squares, held together by a large ornamental safety-pin.

Then I had my hair set, not at the usual place in Clapham, but a salon in Mayfair called Lucille's, extremely expensive and not really me at all. I record all this because I don't wish to spare myself. It was a thoroughly vain performance. I wanted to impress him — of course I did! He was, after all, one of the most attractive young men in the world. There have been several International Polls which agree with this statement.

[*Pause*]

The next day I turned up at the Savoy Hotel in a fair condition of nerves, I have to admit. He opened the door of his suite wearing a Turkish-towel bathrobe, and smiled at me as if we were old, old friends. His skin was *glowing* exactly as it had done in front of the cinema: that dimple was in its place, and his handshake was what I'd call heartfelt . . .

'The scullions have prepared a banquet,' he said. 'Behold! A real Showbiz brunch!'

And there on the table were great plates of smoked salmon and cream cheese, and poached eggs in hollandaise sauce! I was simply inundated with food! . . .

But as soon as I sat down to eat it, he started plying me with the most serious questions – no jokes at all. How much I earned, and whether I could use a computer. It was all very searching, and I couldn't for the life of me see where it was leading, until he suddenly came right out with it, and I almost fainted.

'Angela,' he says, looking extremely earnest and boyish, 'I have a proposition for you . . . How would you like to

19

come to Los Angeles and work for me, at the Rehab. Centre?'

I can tell you, Time just stopped. The film, which I sometimes imagine as my life, became a freeze.

'I'm serious,' he says. 'Don't just say "no" without thinking.' And then he mentioned a sum I couldn't believe. About six times what I was making out of Swift Scripts Limited.

'I want you to supervise the Admissions Department,' he said. 'You'd be responsible for organising a typing pool, just like you do here. And looking after the indexes and the files. You'd have an apartment of your own, right there in the building, on the top floor. "The Penthouse".'

I was completely astounded. 'There must be a thousand women in Los Angeles who can do that work,' I said.

'Ah, but not English!' he said. 'English is different. It'll make people know we're a serious organisation.' Then he grinned at me very shyly and said, 'O.K. Let me fess up!' I'd never heard that expression before – 'fess up': it was enchanting. 'I have always had this mega-fantasy to have a real English Lady Assistant. One of those Margaret Rutherford types, at her desk first thing in the morning with a cheery smile. "Good morning, Mr Prance" – she'd have to say "Prahnce" not "Prairnce" — "and what a jolly morning it is, to be sure!" '

I wasn't entirely delighted to be thought of as a Margaret Rutherford type, but he was so eager and flattering, I hadn't the heart to protest. 'I can tell already you're made for this work,' he said. 'Mega-efficient! Mega-honest! Mega-caring! . . . Maybe you could even do some personal interviewing with the patients!'

How could anyone resist? I just sat there eating hollandaise off the spoon and let him talk me into it . . . Mega, mega, mega — that was me! Who'd have thought it? . . . To be honest, I had always had a mega-fantasy myself, concerning Los Angeles. I suppose like many English people. Sun and palm trees and ice tinkling in tall glasses . . . Actually the truth is we *both* had our fantasies and they coincided. I went to California to lie on *chaise longues* in beach attire — and he asked me there to wear tweeds and say 'How jolly!' And neither of these things occurred . . . If only what did had been that harmless . . .

[*Pause*]

Connie was beyond fury when I told her I was going. She said a great deal more than 'Alas' on this occasion. She told me I'd betrayed our joint venture on a childish whim. It's what she called it and she was partly right, of course — although I did sense a terrific envy under her high moral tone which made it not entirely honest . . . Anyway, I've already apologised for that now, and she did pretty well out of it financially. I made my share of the business over to her for extremely little . . . That's true, Connie, and you know it. It was my way of saying 'sorry'. Hang on — more of this entrancing drink.

[*Pause. She drinks*]

Well that taste really doesn't get any better. Of course it's not likely to do with me — being a Grape person. Grain is my mortal enemy. Ha, ha: joke! Anyway let's get on to California and all the rottenness . . . I flew over the pole. It took nearly eleven hours. I was wildly nervous, of course. After all, I'd now burnt all my bridges and was absolutely on my own. All the same, I had this deep feeling of faith. That's the thing. Whatever happened, Tom would look after me. He was so obviously that kind of person: his frankness and sweetness were really so clear.

I was met at Los Angeles Airport by an alarming figure. A long, lean fellow about thirty-five, badly shaven, and with those weird sunglasses made of mirror-glass on the out-side, so other people can see only themselves. I saw a middle-aged woman who'd been travelling for ages and looked a real mess. Mega-unappetising, if you wanted to describe it. If Tom had appeared then and said to me what I'd said to him outside the cinema — 'You look horrible!' — I wouldn't have blamed him one bit. This was clearly the attitude of the man who'd come in his place: — 'How on earth could anyone have hired this woman?'

I extended my hand but he didn't take it. He just said, 'I'm Bud. Tom's Personal Assistant' — and led me out to a waiting car, about ten feet long, and bright orange. He threw my two cases into the boot with what seemed to me a kind of hostility.

He didn't speak a word all the way in: just kept chewing on a match-stick he had thrusting out of his mouth. I tried to make conversation — said how enormous the roads seemed to be after England — but he just grunted. We got to the Rehabilitation Centre — which was a really smart, white building surrounded by flower beds — and he took me straight upstairs by lift to my flat on the top floor. I was delighted to enter it. I don't know what I'd been expecting, but this was extremely attractive, and even feminine. It occurred to me that Tom had perhaps had it re-decorated for me — it would have been just like him. The walls were pale pink, and there was a large squashy sofa in the middle, covered with a luscious pattern of strawberries all intertwined. I said to Bud 'Well really this is a mega-surprise!' But he simply grunted again — 'Uh', like that — dropped a key on the table and left. I was to hear that 'Uh' quite a lot in future times. It seemed virtually all he could muster by way of personal observation.

I remember that was the afternoon I first met Karen, who was to be my helper. She turned up, all red hair and bright eyes, to give me a tour of the Centre. I must say she was to prove a proper friend — for what that's worth. It was obvious as we went round it the Centre was really a

serious place. Big bright rooms everywhere filled with
people doing Counselling and Group Sessions: I was very
impressed. My own office was wonderfully cheerful and
open-plan: utterly different from our dowdy little hole in
Oxford Street. Not for the first time I thought how we
really *like* dowdiness in England. It's absolutely incurable
in us, I believe. Anyway, in half an hour I won't be part of
it anymore . . .

I saw Tom that same evening. Bud came back and drove
me to his house — and there he suddenly was, sun-tanned
and grinning at me: well, you know that grin, it's in all the
photos. For the first time I felt I was absolutely right to
come! . . . I must say I was delighted with his home — my
first glimpse of real film-star luxury, like my fantasy.
White pebbly walls and a cocktail bar longer than the car —
although why he needed it I couldn't think, since no one
then or ever seemed to drink anything but Diet
Coke . . . Well, all except Bud, that is. He was definitely a
Grain person. He sat about glaring through those mirror
glasses and drinking whisky in what were obviously
enormous quantities. Which reminds me — keep at it,
Angela. You only have to do it once, and so come on:
knock it back!

[*She drinks*]

Good girl. Worthy of Bud, I'd say. Grim Mr Bud . . . I
must say he was a real worry right from the start . . . I
could never make out what he actually did as Tom's
Assistant. Apart from driving him in the car he never

seemed to work at all. Tom on the other hand never stopped. He was making his latest film — *Olly and Ally* — and he'd have to get up at five every single morning. He'd be absolutely worn out when he left the Studio, but this never stopped him coming to see me on his way home. Every night — every single night he'd look in on me in my little penthouse — and always the same performance! I'd hear the lift door open, then the knock — Ba, ba, ba, *ba* — like the Fifth Symphony — and as soon as I opened it, the same cavalierish thing out of his mouth: 'Are you receiving Picture Performers tonight, my lady?'

Then he'd go straight to the fridge for a Diet Coke, throw himself on the sofa, dangle his feet up over the side of it in their green and white gym shoes — and fall backwards among the strawberries, saying? 'Talk! — talk! — talk!' like a Royal command. 'Say anything! I just love to hear English spoken properly!' . . .

He did too. He was a real Anglophile in every way. He'd read every one of Dickens' novels — that was a great source of pride — and he practised calligraphy for half an hour every day. Not that that has anything to do with England, necessarily, but it shows style, you can see that. 'I've always tried all my life,' he used to say, 'not to be a slob! That's the main trouble with the two nations: bad Brits are snobs, bad Americans are slobs. Well I'm not! Tommy never never never shall be a slob!' . . . Which is how he came of course to speak so eloquently — all that 'Whom'. Self-taught, absolutely . . . Well, of course, it had to be — that soon became apparent. His mother had

25

simply abandoned him at birth, and life in American orphanages isn't exactly Dickens and calligraphy. He'd been sent quite young to a farming family — 'farmed to a farm', as he put it — and obviously made to work terribly hard. I imagined him sitting up in a hayloft after a long day's toil in the field reading *Martin Chuzzlewit* by the light of an oil lamp: it was really very moving and somehow very American . . . No wonder when he was spotted he was a Talent Scout's dream.

We talked about everything those evenings. I didn't myself have so much to contribute — in fact to be honest, I was always afraid I'd dry up and he wouldn't come any more: after all, weekends in Clapham and holidays in Torquay aren't exactly holding subjects. I was forced in fact to be cunning — as anyone would try to be in my position, faced with the world's most attractive listener . . . I started to get involved with the patients at the Clinic.

It wasn't hard. Californians love to discuss their emotional problems — it's actually their favourite occupation — and I made an absolutely wonderful listener, shameful as it may be to say so. Each day I spent more and more time listening, and less and less with my dreary filing cards, till I was virtually counselling — just like a qualified psychiatrist! Tom didn't mind at all. 'Qualifications don't matter' he'd say. 'All they want really is a Mom: a real old-fashioned Mom to look after them. And that's who you are, Angie! — that's who you really are: Super-Mom!' . . .

I found that so beautiful − even though it was actually absurd as I was quite obviously in fact nobody's Mom and wasn't ever going to be . . . Of course, being an orphan, I suppose it wasn't hard to see why he had need for someone like myself.

The weird thing about our evening sessions was that Bud would drive Tom to them in the orange car, and then wait outside in it for however long they took − never coming in himself. I'd look down from my window and see him sitting there at the wheel, just staring ahead through his mirror-glasses and chewing his match-stick, like some kind of sinister chauffeur. I'd ask Tom if he wouldn't rather come up and join us, but he'd always say, 'No: leave him. He's happy. Bud's a loner.' Of course I was being hypocritical asking, since I didn't really want him in my flat at all. I was sublimely happy the way things were − just Tom and me, and my nightly reports on the patients. Over three months I became as expert as anybody in giving therapy − I don't mind saying it. They were mostly teenagers, but there were housewives as well, and older. One heroin addict was actually sixty-three! The work was hard and I did it well, I know it. *I had a role* − a proper role! − and proper commonsensical things to say. I had help to give for the first time − that's it, you see: *proper* work! . . .

And always at the end of the day, *him* − Tom Beautiful Prance, to hear of it − like a visiting . . . well, a visiting young god.

He really did seem − soppy as it is to say it − to get more handsome each day. There are naturally handsome people who actually improve the more they leave adolescence and journey out on the sea of life.

One night when he called I was for once more exhausted than he. A young girl had had hysterics on the third floor, and tried to throw herself out of the window. I'd had to hold her for quite a long time, till the medical people arrived − and there was a pain right across my shoulders from the strain. Tom made me lie down on the sofa, face downwards, on the pattern of strawberries. And then he put his hands on me, and began to massage my back. The feeling was amazing. I swear, within one minute the pain started to go. And when I looked up, obviously extremely grateful because it had really been agony, his face was just one inch from mine. Before I could stop myself, I kissed his dimple: quite briskly − really, really matter-of-factly − but it was still like kissing satin. His skin *was* satin! The message was absolutely plain to me. Whatever else I felt for him, it wasn't what Super-Mom should feel! . . . And then he spoke to me in the softest voice.

'You're a fantastic person, Angie. And I hope you'll be here forever.'

Then he helped me up and I said, 'Yes. I will be. If you wish it.'

It was after that he made the confession to me. When he was in his teens he had taken drugs himself — quite a few. He'd been helped to get off them by an older person. This was really why he had started the Centre — to help others in his turn . . .

I ought to have guessed — nothing that happened to him was just left, you know. It had to be turned to good . . . When he told me the story he hugged me for a second to his chest — and then left the room, very churned up inside. And of course I was churned up too.

[*Pause*]

And that was the beginning with hugs. He was really a hugger in a big way: some are, some aren't.

And for me, of course, it was absolutely a new sensation. My husband, poor Arthur, never touched at all, let alone hugged or stroked. He saved all his stroking for the billiard cue . . . I didn't imagine Bud was much of a hugger either: those simply weren't hugger's hands. They were for mending car engines, and pouring whisky. I soon gave up my attempts to appease him – which wasn't exactly difficult because you can't really appease images of yourself staring anxiously out of little mirrors on a sneering, unshaven man's face. But ignoring him wasn't really so easy . . . For one thing he'd turn up at my door every couple of days bearing the cassette of an old film. The thing was I had a television with a VCR machine, and Tom would send him over with all the old classics for me taken out of his huge library dating back to Charlie Chaplin and Buster Keaton. He used to do the most perfect imitation of Chaplin with a cane and bowler: I'd laugh so much I'd hurt. One day a filling actually shot out of one of my teeth as I was laughing. He picked it up and refused to give it back. 'That's an oldie but goldie!' he said . . .

Well, anyway, Bud would come round with the films, always just pushing them at me as soon as I opened the door, and then sort of lounging back into the lift without a word, except of course for that 'Uh' . . .

I realise now it was actually his total lack of manners that made me treat him the way I did when it came to the point. If I'd liked him more I'd have been more merciful. Of course I would! . . .

[*Pause*]

It all exploded one lunch hour. Actually under a week ago, incredible to believe . . . Tom had offered to lend me *Lost Horizon* in the original version with Ronald Colman, and I told him if Bud dropped it off during the lunch hour, when I always ate my home-prepared banana sandwiches in the flat — much preferring them to the canteen with its nasty smelly tuna fish — I'd be there to receive the film. Imagine my surprise when I went up there at one o'clock to find Bud actually ensconced inside the room! He was lying on the sofa with his feet up! — exactly as Tom would lie when he came for his Diet Coke. Except Bud wasn't drinking Diet Coke, or anything else. He'd obviously had a key to the flat all the time I was in residence, and even more obviously had chosen this place — my living room — *on purpose*, to do what he was doing.

I couldn't believe my eyes. I knew what they were seeing at once — my new knowledge of drugs told me that. Round his arm was a thin strap tied tight, and in it a needle from a syringe. There was blood coming back into it, and on the table, beside my plate of sandwiches, was all the paraphernalia, and the remnants of the powder . . .

It was hideous. He was actually lying there on my sofa — injecting! . . . *Shooting up*, as they call it! . . . His awful mirror-glasses were off for the first time, and I saw his eyes: they were pale, pale grey as if he lived in the dark all the time, and completely unfocussed . . . I heard myself letting out absurd noises — 'Oh' and 'Ah' and 'Oooh' — not making any real words. And he just leering at me and saying 'Home. Home Sweet Home! *My* sweet home, Angela! My little pink pad! . . . You borrowed it, girl, but it's mine: understand that!' . . .

31

'Girl!' — imagine that coming out of a leering, dribbling face! . . . My legs were trembling so badly I could hardly stand up — I rushed out into the lift and away — straight down to the canteen to find help — Karen my Assistant. I pulled her up by the arm, I said 'Drive me to the Studio! Right now!'

The orange car was waiting where Bud had left it — the key still in. I just said. 'Take it!' and pushed her into it . . . We drove along that awful Freeway — I sat there trembling — it wouldn't stop for a moment. There was a Guard at the Studio gate, but he saw the Pass on the windscreen and waved us through. Karen knew exactly where to find Tom.

We went right up to a heavy metal door with a red light shining overhead: no one was to go in while it was on — it meant they were shooting. I didn't care: I just ignored it. I went straight through on to the set — lights blazing and technicians all around looking at me astounded. I can see it still now — just like a film unrolling. The set was meant to be a tropical beach, with fake palm trees in a circle, and Tom in the middle wearing a tiny bathing suit, his whole body made up bright orange — like the colour of his car. Suddenly I was just there in front of him, shouting in his face and someone angry was calling out 'Cut! . . . Cut! . . . '

I still can't believe I did it. It felt just as if we were both in a tremendous film together about tropical passion — the camaras turning, and all the workers around just gaping at the intensity of what we were doing! . . . But I wasn't acting. It was absolutely real. Real! I could hear my words rushing out − swearing and everything − not able to stop: damn and damn and damn! 'Damn him − your Bud! Your damn Bud! Your Personal Assistant! . . . Do you know what he's doing? Where he actually is now − this moment? . . . On your sofa! My sofa! *Mine*! with a needle in his arm!'

He just stood there goggling, and I went on shouting and shouting till they got me out. Hustled me − a guard, some black man with an actual gun on his hip tugged me along a corridor and out into a taxi − threw me, hard, onto the back seat! . . .

[*Pause*]

When I got home, Bud was gone. Only the needle was left on the table as a final insult − stuck through my pile of sandwiches.

[*Long pause*]

Tom didn't come that night. I began to phone, over and over, but couldn't ever find the courage to actually finish dialling.

And then the next day very early the doorbell rang. I rushed to answer − but instead it was Bud standing there

– the glasses back on his face – simply holding another
film cassette. I'd no idea why, at eight in the morning. He
pushed it into my hand, and I just slammed the door. I
remember standing there for a second after he'd gone
thinking, 'Oh no. Something dreadful is now about to
happen. What is this film? Even its feel is rotten – the
actual feel . . . ' The sensation of being in a film myself
was still with me, but the kind of film had changed. Now
it was the beastly kind – a woman on her own in a house
and something awful about to happen.

And then I put on one, and saw what he wanted me to
see . . . The room. That very room I was actually in, with
the sofa and the strawberry pattern. And there on it – tied
up on it – over it – like a captive – was Tom. Naked. He
was wearing some kind of harness, made of leather, with
studs on it. And behind him, leaning over, was Bud –
holding up what I first thought was a stick. But then I saw
it wasn't . . . And what was worse – much worse – was
the joy on Tom's face, the wicked joy! . . . . There was
obviously a third person doing the filming, and as the
camera came in close Tom grinned, as if to me – but with
such *relish*! . . . Reared back and grinned and flicked his
tongue – *as if to me*! . . .

And as I watched, there was laughter, coming in under the
door! A man was laughing! . . . I rushed over and threw it
open – and there was a pile of more films on the mat –
about a dozen – and Bud standing across in the lift,

grinning too . . . 'Some more for your viewing pleasure' he said, and pressed the button and disappeared.

[*Long pause*]

I didn't go down to work that day. Or the next one. I didn't go anywhere. The Centre must have wondered where I was, but no one came up to inquire. Not even Karen . . [*Pause*] I must have looked ghastly when Tom finally came to see me. I could see it in his face. Not even distress — disgust!

I found myself saying, 'I'm sorry.' . . . Imagine it! 'I'm sorry' — to him! Just because I hadn't combed my hair and was still wearing the clothes I had on two days before, when Bud brought the film.

I don't know what happened to the pile left on the mat outside. The one I'd played was lying where I'd left it, by the television. He came in, all stiff and solemn: sat on the sofa like a Judge. Then used a voice I'd never heard before. Icy cold. Cruel-cold: that kind.

'This is bad. Real bad. You shouldn't have done it, Angela.' Angela now — not Angie.

'What?' I say. 'Done what exactly?'

'What you did, in the studio,' he says. 'Everyone heard you. All the camera guys. Now it's all over the place.'

'Well that's too bad,' I say.

'It is,' he says. 'It's very bad. Everyone's talking.'

Suddenly it's my fault, you see. It's not what *he* did — what *I* did! He's looking at me remotely — that marvellous face sort of stone, absolute stone! I feel I have to defend myself — only I can't get the words out . . . I tried, of course. I said 'Listen — it's your work — your work that's been demeaned! Think where it took place — your Centre! No one can come into that and take drugs, I don't care who it is — not in here! No one!'

Then he holds up his hand for silence, and says: 'Angela, listen. This room is not part of the Centre, even if it's in the same building. The truth is, I should never have given it to you. It was really *his* room. I told him I'd like you to have it and he didn't object, but I ought to have known he would. It's his *act* to be cool — not to show he resents anything. But he must have done . . . We used to come here and talk, him and me, on this sofa. It meant something to him, this room — I ought to have imagined that. Failure of imagination, Angela — that's the whole trouble with the world.'

36

Whom Do I Have the Honour of Addressing?

Can you believe it? . . . 'Talk!' – 'come here and *talk*,' that's what he said! . . . Clearly he'd no idea what I had seen . . . He just sat there looking all pained and Jesussy, talking about failure of imagination! And about Bud – what a great guy he was! 'You should have known him before. He was so different – so beautiful! He was the one who got me off drugs. The older person I told you about. He virtually saved my life – then went on them himself when you came. The stupid guy!' . . . He was jealous, you see. He's weak that way.'

Wonderful! . . . It was all my fault! Bud had done no-thing! I was insensitive, interfering Angela – but he was just poor Bud, poor weak guy I'd driven on to drugs. It was unbelievable! . . . It was actually *intolerable!* . . . And then he went on, as if this wasn't enough – 'Please understand one thing. I'm fond of you, Angela, but he has to be my priority. If push comes to shove he's the one who stays.'

As if there was some sort of competition between us! And that awful expression, 'push and shove'! . . . I couldn't stand it anymore – the whole thing was disintegrating right there – falling away all round – leaving nothing for me in the world, and Nobody there looking at me – just a kind of stone-faced boy . . .

And then he puts on one of those really beastly smiles, those hippy smiles, you know – all lofty and superior and 'With-It', and he says 'Oh Angela!' – Just like that – like a

Bishop, suddenly! – 'Oh Angela: why is it so difficult? Why can't we all live together in Peace? Why do we have to wound each other? . . . There was no need for you to have been that cruel to him. To be his Judge. Nobody is any person's Judge. Remember that.'

And then I just snap – like that!

'I'll be what I please,' I say. 'What I damn please! I'm no Californian hypocrite – goody-good on top and filth underneath! I know when I've been mocked and abused – because that's it really – just *mockery!* Margaret Ruther-ford sitting so prim on the sofa – *that sofa!* – ha ha, what a joke!' . . .

And then it happens before I know it. I couldn't help it – I wasn't really aware . . . I just reached down and picked up that filthy film in its metal case and shoved it at him – *real* push and shove this time! I think he recognised it – in that second his eyes went wide – and then I slashed him with it hard, right across the brow with the edge of the case, and his forehead just opened up, like a zipper parting. He gave a scream – exactly like a girl – and shot up off the sofa and ran to the mirror! . . . It was all he could think of – instantly! – *what he looked like!* What damage had been done to that famous, beautiful face!

[*Pause*]

38

Whom Do I Have the Honour of Addressing?

The cut was really deep, I could tell. He stood staring at himself with the blood running down fast in a fringe, like one of those disgusting holy pictures of the Crown of Thorns. And then he turned to me and said — said to me, so quietly I could hardly hear it: 'Bitch . . . F. Bitch You F. Bitch.' Yes.

And then it all went out of control. As if the film we were both in was suddenly jumping off the spool! Out of the machine and into the air — suddenly flapping and slapping all over the floor — only it was me on the floor, with noise everywhere! Me screaming and him screaming down at me with blood tassels hanging off his head — and his mouth opening and shutting, driving words into me — terrible, terrible words! — driving them hard! It's not true when they say sticks and stones — words hurt much more! Much, much, much! . . . I never knew he could speak like that — all the Dickens forgotten, and the 'Whom' . . . Now he was just running round the room screaming — And the blood was dripping on to his gym shoes — red drops splashing on the green and white, going round and round . . . And that was the last thing I did see. It all went away suddenly.

[Long pause]

[*calmer*] I never saw him afterwards. I woke up lying on the sofa, with a rug on me. And then I slept again for several hours, and finally Bud was standing over me, holding an air ticket. 'You're going,' he said. 'Now.'

My cases were standing in the doorway. Someone had packed for me, I suppose Karen. I got up like an auto-maton and walked out of my flat down in the lift to the orange car. There was no one about at all. The Centre looked deserted — as if they'd all been given the day off to avoid meeting me.

Bud drove me to the airport. Evening, with the lights. He just kept staring at the road. And when we got to that enormous place with all the travellers being set down, he simply stopped and waited for me to get out and lift my own cases. And then drove on without a look. I was left to find a trolley myself. Which was actually better. Being helped would have made it all much worse. I kept thinking all sorts of personal belongings had probably been left behind in the flat. But what did it matter?

[*Long pause. The whisky is starting to have its effect, more and more insistently*]

I'm dizzy now. It's not very agreeable . . . I'm sitting here looking at those cases right now. I still haven't unpacked them. Two days. Two days in joyous Clapham. I can see their labels from here — the original ones for California: 'Care of The Pranceway Rehabilitation Centre, Los Angeles' . . . Not much point in opening them. Other

people will do that. The police, or whoever. They'll have to break the door down, I suppose . . . What will they say when they hear this tape? I can predict absolutely! 'Silly bitch! . . . Silly F. Bitch! What a stupid thing to do — for a boy nearly young enough to be her grandson! Why didn't she just stay in London where she belonged?' . . . Anyway, that's it. I'm going to stop it now. The tape's almost at an end, and there's no sense turning it over to the other side. I'm a One-side person, really, like everybody else: there's not many people in the world worth two . . . So stop right here!

[*She stops the machine*]

Oh, I am dizzy. It's hard to think exactly . . . Leave the note — that's the important thing: just three little words: 'Please Play This'. And then these.

[*She rattles the pills in their bottle*]

Ten little bombs. Down the throat — and that'll be it. Then the fun starts for everyone else! . . . Especially you. Poor Tom. You're going to be famous in quite a different way. I wouldn't want to be you when all this is published! All those newspapers and Fan Mags! — 'Tom Prance In Suicide Scandal!' . . . 'Film Star's Life of Kink!' . . . [*She laughs*] That'll show you, won't it? What we can do if we choose — we Margaret Rutherford types! . . . You're going to be ruined, Satin-Face! All those journalists are going to have such fun with you — those charming English journalists — can't you just hear them ringing up their editors? 'You know that Goody-good, always lecturing kids about the Pure Life? Well, we've got the goody-

41

goods on him, alright!' . . . [*She laughs again*] It'll be the
end of you, my dear! Just this one tiny tape here — that's
all it'll need, and bye-bye to you — Mr Knight of the Fur
Coat! . . .

[*But suddenly she cries out*]

Oh no! . . . No, no, no, no, no! . . . I *can't!* . . . At least
you have something — *a smile!* What have *they* got? —
Bloody Fleet Street Nothings?! Just envy! English envy!
Damn English malice! . . .

[*Pause*]

I can't do it. Not this way. You don't deserve that,
whatever else! . . . I'll save you, Tom! I will. I promise!
I'll protect you! Look — all I'd have to do is re-wind —
look, see here, this button! — and when it's all back, just
press 'Record' again — the tape will turn and everything
will go. They'll find nothing! The only place it'll be will be
our heads . . . Your lovely head — with that gash on it
now. That's not going to heal so easily, is it? — it's too
deep. You'll have plastic surgery, and perhaps it won't
work. Then you'll have it for life. And that'll be the end of
your career — without any tape being necessary
. . . How weird. I always thought of myself as harmless.
No one is, you see.

[*Pause*]

[*More tenderly*] All right: let me do it. I've done you
enough damage: you don't need any more from me. Wipe
it all off. The pills will just have to wait till that's done.

42

Re-wind — then erase. My final present to you.

[*She presses the 'Re-wind' button and the babble of the tape running in reverse is heard loudly*]

Listen. D'you know what that is? The sound of life going backwards! . . . If only it could! Back to the time before I hit you — no, before I met you! before 'Whom!' — that silly Cavalier's voice: 'Whom do I have the honour of addressing?' . . . Oh, Tommy! What will you say when you hear about it? I bet I can predict that too. [*American*] 'Did ya hear? She's dead, that English woman? I guess she musta done it for *me*!' . . . [*Her own voice*] That's it, isn't it? I bet that's what you'll say. [*American*] 'Poor bitch, she did it for *me*!' — Tom Prance the Beautiful! . . . [*Her own voice*] Oh no. We can't have that, my dear. Whatever else, not that! That's just too *much* of a present. It really is, my dimply friend. It's enough to have your life given back to you — you don't have to smirch mine as well!

[*Pause*]

I'll tell you what. Why don't I just hold off on the bombs for a bit? — stay alive and be a torment to you? A little nasty Miss Rutherford sitting in Clapham, able to speak at any time! How about that instead? Miss Sword of Damocles! Angela Damocles of old Los Angeles! . . . It'll make you both so nervous! [*American voice*] 'Hey Bud, what's she thinkin' about over there in London, all alone in that crummy Clap-ham? You realise she could sell her story to the press at any time – what she knows about us! . . . Listen — listen — maybe I should send you over to London to take care of her. You know — rub her out.' [*Laughing, in her own voice*] He would, too, wouldn't he? I'll look out of the window one night and there he'll be, looking up — mirror-glasses glinting in the moonlight! . . . One of those murdering-lonely-women films, like *Sorry, Wrong Number*, with Barbara Stanwyck! . . . [*Desperate*] Oh God, I'm awful! Just awful! Stupid! I'm rotten, Tommy! . . . I'm mad!

[*The babble comes up in volume and the tape stops with a click*]

So what is it, then? Stay or go? Perhaps I should just go back to the office — dear old Wardour Street. Knock on the door with a flourish — dear old Fifth Symphony — Ba-ba-ba-Ba! [*cheerful voice*] 'Hullo everyone! I'm back! I missed you all so much, I just couldn't keep away! Especially you, Connie! . . . You haven't a job for me, by any chance? Just regular typing — I'm sure you wouldn't want a partner again, ha, ha, ha! It would just be so nice to be working at Swift Scripts once again!' . . .

[*Prissy voice*] 'Ah, well now, Angela, there really is nothing available here at this exact moment. Alas! I'm so very sorry. Things are a bit difficult just now, alas.' . . . Alo-alas-alat! . . . [*desperately*] Tell me, Tommy, seriously — what am I going to do? As if you know. Or care.

[*Pause*]

There's a spot of blood on my sweater. When you ran round the room, one drop fell on me — from your head. Right here: on my breast. If I'm still here tomorrow I'll take it to the cleaners. If I'm not — who will ever know what it is? . . . First things first: take *us* to the cleaners. Wipe us all away. Then at least you'll be safe from me, if I decide to do it. Goodbye, Tom. Press 'Record' again. And goodbye — my visiting god.

[*She presses the 'Record' button. Then she speaks intimately into the machine*]

Hallo . . . Hallo . . . Hallo . . . Whom . . . Whom . . . Whom . . .

[*Pause*]

Whom do I have the honour of erasing?

[*She gives a faint laugh*]

[*The music returns: 'When you wish upon a star' arranged for sweet and swirling strings.*]

[END]